THE BOY WHO LOVED TO DRAW

Benjamin West

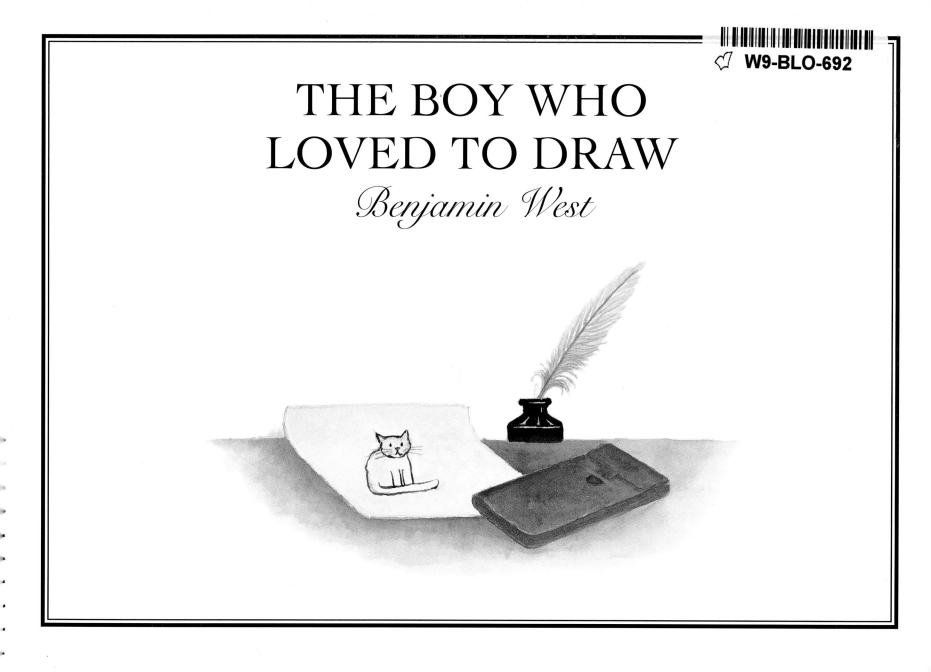

For my husband, Fred,

who was a boy who loved to draw

— B.B.

For Ed and Kelly, of course

— O.D.

The text of this book is set in 16-point Cochin.
The illustrations are gouache on paper.

Library of Congress Cataloging-in-Publication Data

Brenner, Barbara.
The boy who loved to draw: Benjamin West / Barbara Brenner ; illustrated by Olivier Dunrea.
p. cm.
Summary: Recounts the life story of the Pennsylvania artist who began drawing as a boy
and eventually became well known on both sides of the Atlantic.
ISBN 0-395-85080-0
1. West, Benjamin, 1738–1820 — Juvenile literature. 2. Painters—United States — Biography — Juvenile literature.
[1. West, Benjamin, 1738–1820. 2. Artists.] I. Dunrea, Olivier, ill.
II. Title.
ND237.W45B74 1999
759.13—dc21
[B]   97-5183 CIP AC

Printed in Singapore
TWP 10 9 8 7 6 5 4 3 2 1

THE BOY WHO LOVED TO DRAW

Benjamin West

Barbara Brenner

Illustrated by Olivier Dunrea

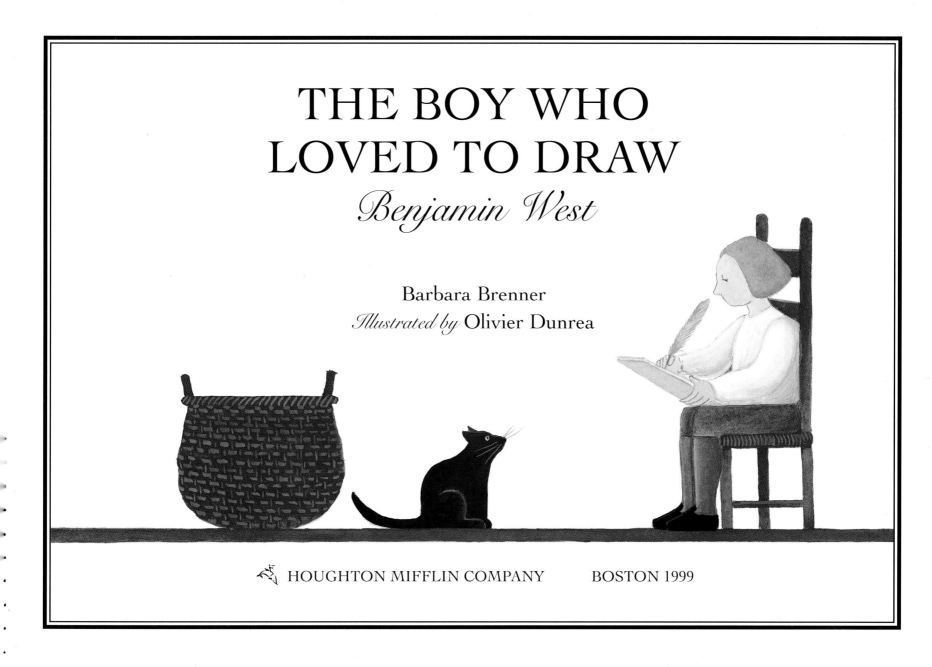

HOUGHTON MIFFLIN COMPANY   BOSTON 1999

The Wests of Pennsylvania were a houseful.
First there were Mama and Papa.
Then came John and Thomas, Samuel and Joseph,
Rachel and Sarah. Then Hannah, Mary, and Elizabeth.
And then there was Benjamin.

Benjamin was number ten. He came along in 1738.
When he was born, the preacher said about him,
"This boy will do great things someday."
But he never did say exactly how or when.
So everyone kept an eye on Benjamin,
waiting for the first signs of greatness.

CHAPTER ONE

A SIGN

*W*hen Benjamin was seven, a sign did show.
It happened one day while his married sister
was visiting. Rachel had brought her new baby
with her. She asked Benjamin to tend little Sally
while she and Mama went for a walk.
Benjamin made a sour face, but Rachel told him,
"She's asleep. All you have to do is
rock the cradle and flap the flies away."

So Rachel and Mama went for their walk.
Benjamin rocked and flapped and wished
mightily that he was doing something else.

To help pass the time, he studied his little niece's face.
He had never seen a new baby up so close.
How tiny her nose was! What long eyelashes she had!
And then, quite suddenly, Benjamin West became possessed
of a powerful itch.
He wanted to draw a picture of that baby!

He knew he'd have to be quick about it.

Mama and Rachel would be back any minute.

He looked around for something to draw with.

There was Papa's goose quill on the desk.

But, *hold on!* No one but Papa was supposed

to use that quill pen!

For a minute Benjamin's hand stayed in the air.

Then he reached for the pen and dipped it in the inkwell.

After that Benjamin forgot all about Papa's rules.

He forgot all about rocking and flapping.

He forgot about everything but drawing that picture.

The drawing was almost finished when the baby woke up.

She started to fuss. Benjamin rocked the cradle as hard as he could

but little Sally cried louder and louder.

Now Benjamin heard voices in the garden.

Mama and Rachel were coming back! Benjamin left off rocking, dropped the quill back into the inkwell, and snatched up his drawing.

Just then Mama and Rachel rushed in. Rachel ran to the cradle to pick up the baby, but Mama's sharp eyes were on Benjamin. "Benjamin West! What's that you're hiding behind your back?"

Benjamin could feel his face getting hot.

He handed over the drawing.

Then he squeezed his eyes shut so he wouldn't have to watch Mama looking at it.

Benjamin wished he could shut his ears, too.

He knew Mama was going to say, "Foolishness!"

And she was going to ask about the pen!

It was quiet in the room for a long time.
Then Mama said softly,
"Rachel, looky here. Benjamin has made a picture
of our little Sally."

Benjamin opened his eyes. His mama and Rachel were staring at
his drawing, and they were both smiling!
"I declare, it looks just like her," Rachel said.
She turned to Benjamin. "How ever did you do that, child?"
Benjamin shrugged and tried to look modest,
like a proper Quaker boy. But inside, he was bursting with pride.
Mama and Rachel liked his drawing!

That night Mrs. West said to Mr. West,
"Father, I do believe Benjamin's drawing is a sign."
Mr. West said, "You may be right, Mother. Time will tell."

CHAPTER TWO
INDIANS

*F*rom that day on, you never saw Benjamin West without a pen and notebook. While other boys were spending their spare time fishing or pitching horseshoes, Benjamin West was drawing pictures. He'd draw anything his eye lit on—squirrel or cow, house or tree.

A year went by. One day Benjamin was sitting
by the river, drawing a robin. He began to have a feeling
that eyes were watching him. What was back there in those woods?
Bear? Wolf? Maybe it was *Meesing,* the ghost the Indians told about.

Benjamin turned around ever so slowly. He looked over his
shoulder. In the shadows he could see three faces. *Indians!*
The hair prickled on the back of his neck.
Were they friendly Lenapes?
Or were they some of those fierce Shawnees from the west?

Benjamin sat still as a stone. After what seemed a long time,
one Indian came out of the woods.

Benjamin shouted with relief, "Gray Wolf!"

Gray Wolf was a Lenape, and a friend. His wigwam was near the West house.

Gray Wolf and his family often came to sell Indian baskets to the guests at Papa's inn.

Gray Wolf and Benjamin shook hands solemnly.

As if that was a signal, the other Indians stepped out of the woods.

They looked at Benjamin's bird drawing.

They waved their arms around and talked excitedly in Lenape.

"*Meesh-ka, meesh-ka,*" they kept saying.

"What's *meesh-ka*?" Benjamin asked Gray Wolf.

Gray Wolf pointed to the robin's breast.

"*Meesh-ka* means 'It is red.' The bird should be red on the breast."

"I know that," Benjamin said, trying not to sound peevish.

"But I have no red paint."

Gray Wolf looked puzzled. "Paint? Paint?" Suddenly he said, "Ah! Paint! You want paint—you come!"

Gray Wolf led Benjamin along the riverbank

while the other Indians trailed behind.

They came to a place where the riverbank was all red clay.

Gray Wolf handed Benjamin a hollow gourd. He pointed.

"Ans-ha," he said, in Lenape. Then, in English, "You take it up."

Benjamin bent down and scooped up the red clay

from the riverbank. Then Gray Wolf led him to a place where

the ground was yellow clay.

"Ans-ha," he said again. Benjamin scooped up the yellow clay.

The Indian put the two lumps of clay into two bowls.

With a long, smooth stone, he ground each lump into powder.

Next he took some bear grease from a leather bag.

He mixed the grease first with the red, then with the yellow clay.

The clay turned into a thick red and yellow paste.

He handed the bowls to Benjamin. "Here is your paint!"

Benjamin ran all the way home.

His mother was waiting at the door.

He called to her excitedly, "Mama! Mama!

Gray Wolf showed me how to make paint!"

But Mama wasn't listening. She was cross.

"Benjamin West, where in creation have you been?

You forgot to feed and water the horses."

Benjamin hung his head.

"I was down by the river, drawing. I . . ."

Again he told her about the Indians and the paint.

When he had finished, his mother sighed.

"Benjamin, I declare, I don't know where this drawing fancy

of yours is going to lead."

Just then she spied Benjamin's drawing of the bird.

A tiny smile began to show at the corners of her mouth.

She walked over to the bowls of paint.

She inspected the contents.

Finally she said, "I reckon you could use one more color."

Mrs. West went to the cupboard and brought out the stick of

blue indigo that she used for dyeing wool.

She handed it to Benjamin, saying,

"Now you have red, yellow, and blue. With those three you can

mix most any other color."

Benjamin West went to bed that night thinking he

was the luckiest boy in all of Lancaster County.

He had colors to paint with!

CHAPTER THREE
THE CAT

*B*ut the next morning Benjamin didn't feel so lucky.

He had no way to get that paint onto his paper.

"Put it on with your fingers," his brother Joseph said.

"Try it with a quill pen," said his brother Samuel.

"Maybe you could use a butter paddle," his sister Mary suggested.

Every one of Benjamin's brothers and sisters had a different idea.

None of the ideas worked.

One day a traveler from Philadelphia was staying at the inn.

He saw Benjamin struggling with the paint.

"What you need is a hair pencil," the man told him.

"What on earth is that?" asked Benjamin.

"It's a goose quill with a camel's-hair brush at the tip.

Artists use it for putting on paint."

Benjamin had never heard of such a thing. But he surely wanted to have one.

He asked the man where he could get a camel's-hair pencil.

"You can buy one in Philadelphia," the traveler told him.

Benjamin had never in his life been as far as Philadelphia.

He guessed he'd have to forget about owning a hair pencil.

He tried. But it was no use. He saw camels and hair pencils in his dreams.

One day Benjamin was drawing a picture

of Grimalkin, the family cat.

He began to have a little conversation with himself.

My! What thick fur Grimalkin has!

A few minutes later, *My! What a bushy tail Grimalkin has.*

Gradually an idea formed in Benjamin's head.

He took up a pair of his mama's scissors.

He found a long goose quill and some yarn.

He called, "Here, Grimalkin. Here, kitty-cat."

Grimalkin had no idea what Benjamin was up to. He came running to his master.

Benjamin grabbed him and quick as lightning snipped some hairs from the cat's tail.

He held the hairs at the tip of the goose quill.

Carefully, he wound the yarn around them.

In a few minutes Benjamin West had made himself a hair pencil.

Sadly, it didn't last long. After a few strokes the homemade

brush fell apart. So Benjamin took up the scissors again.

Once more it was

"Here, Grimalkin! Here, cat!"

The second hair pencil didn't last any longer than the first.

But when Benjamin called a third time, Grimalkin ran and hid under the bed.

After that the cat took to staying in the barn.

When Benjamin needed a new hair pencil,

he had to hunt Grimalkin down.

One day Mr. West spied Grimalkin slinking around the yard.

"What in the world ails our cat?" he asked Benjamin.

"He looks as if moths had been at him."

Benjamin took a long hard look at Grimalkin.

The cat was indeed a sorry sight.

His back end was completely bald

and there were large patches on his sides

where fur was missing.

Benjamin realized how much of Grimalkin was in hair pencils.

"Papa, I did it," he confessed.

He told his father the whole story.

When he had finished, Mr. West pressed his lips together

and walked away, looking very angry.

Benjamin knew punishment was coming.

He didn't know what the punishment would be. A whipping he could stand. But what if Papa forbade him to draw anymore?

When his father came back, his mother was with him. They both looked as sober as judges. Papa started talking. "Benjamin, this drawing and painting—it has such a hold over you. You think of nothing else. It has led you now into mischief. We must act now before you go further. So your mother and I have decided. We are going to send you—"

Benjamin's head felt as if it would burst.

They are going to send me away! This is what happens to wicked boys who don't do their chores and take the fur off their cat's tail. I am being sent away to work! My master may beat and starve me as he pleases!

How could his parents do this to him? Was it such a sin
to love to draw?
Benjamin's eyes filled with tears.
He hardly listened to the rest of what Papa was saying, until
he heard "Philadelphia" and then "artist."

Suddenly he put it together. Benjamin West was not being sent
away to be beaten and starved! He was being sent to
Philadelphia to meet a real live artist! He was going to find
out if he had the makings of a good painter.
Benjamin had a feeling that this trip was going to change his life.

AND THEN WHAT HAPPENED?

The trip did change Benjamin West's life. The "real live artist," William Williams, took a look at Benjamin's work and predicted that if he kept on drawing and painting he would someday be a great painter. That day one very happy nine-year-old boy was given his first box of real paints, "hair pencils," and some canvas.

When Benjamin was twelve years old, he sold his first painting, for one dollar. By the age of eighteen he was doing a thriving business painting portraits in Pennsylvania. But Benjamin decided he didn't want to spend his life doing portraits. He went off to Italy to study art and then settled down in England. By the time Benjamin West was thirty, his work was well known on both sides of the Atlantic Ocean. In the colonies, George and Martha Washington owned one of his paintings. Benjamin Franklin, whose portrait he had painted, was his close friend and the godfather of one of his children.

In England, King George III was an admirer of the paintings of Benjamin West. The king gave West studio space in the palace, and the two men became friends. But when the American colonies rebelled, Benjamin West took sides with the rebels! Some of King George's advisers told him to arrest the American for treason. Surprisingly, the English king stood up for his friend West's right to his opinion. The two remained friends.

Benjamin West lived the rest of his life in England and became rich and famous. But he never forgot his American roots. His door was always open to young artists, especially those from the United States. In fact, Benjamin West, the boy who loved to draw, is often called the father of American art.

Here are a few of his paintings.

Landscape with Cow
(West's first painting, painted at age ten)
Historic Collections,
Pennsylvania Hospital, Philadelphia

Penn's Treaty with the Indians

Courtesy of the Museum of American Art of the Pennsylvania
Academy of the Fine Arts, Philadelphia.
Gift of Mrs. Sarah Harrison (The Joseph Harrison, Jr. Collection)

Portrait of Jane Morris

(Painted at age fourteen)
Chester County Historical Society,
West Chester, Pennsylvania.
Photo credit: George J. Fistrovich

IF YOU WANT TO KNOW MORE

*T*he house where Benjamin West was born is still standing, on the campus of Swarthmore College in Swarthmore, Pennsylvania.

Benjamin West's paintings are in the collections of museums all over the world. Here in the United States you can see his work in the Metropolitan Museum of Art in New York City, the National Gallery of Art in Washington, D.C., and the Philadelphia Museum of Art in Philadelphia, Pennsylvania, among other places.

The material for this book is based mainly on West's own account of his childhood, as told to his biographer, John Galt. I also referred to Robert C. Alberts's 1978 biography, *Benjamin West*. For the information on the language of the Delaware Indians, I am grateful to the Pocono Indian Museum in Bushkill, Pennsylvania.